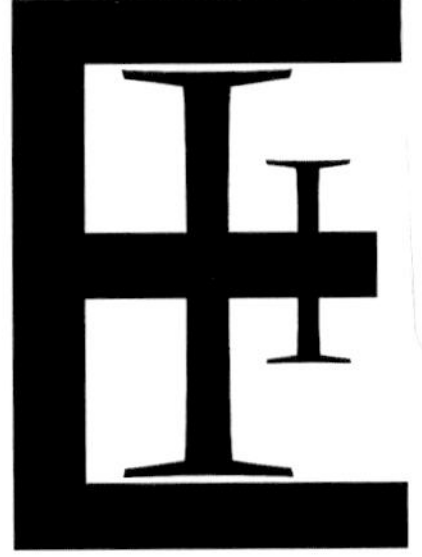

The symbol you see was that of the "Extreme Individual Institute." Now that Dr. Hyatt is gone, the Institute is no more. Beware those who would assert otherwise! Beware the institutes and foundations and any other organization that purports to teach what Dr. Hyatt taught. Only Hyatt was Hyatt. No one else is, or can be.

The goal of the institute was simple: to assist extreme individuals to become who they are.

This work was for that 10% of marginal people who desire to become greater than they are now. It was not a forum or discussion or argument.

The methods of the Institute were simple: "work" in the arena of the obvious as well as the sublime. However, Dr. Hyatt was only concerned with results and not moralisms—what a person does with his power is his business.

Work was done individually via both personal contact and the internet, plus a yearly coming together done either in the physical or on the internet. There was a strict entrance exam and monthly payments were required for the operation of the Institute.

— Nicholas Tharcher

Postscript August 2009: A New EII has appeared on the horizon at http://neweii.com. It appears to be run by former students of Dr. Hyatt and, with all the caveats above, seems to be legitimate. We are keeping a close watch…

Robes — P. Emerson Williams

DR. HYATT'S BLACK BOOK OMEGA

Cirque Apokálypsis

Become Who You Are—There Are No Guarantees

Christopher S. Hyatt, Ph.D.

With your ringmaster
Joseph Matheny

And in the Center Ring

Nick Pell — *Dogma Tamer*

Calvin Iwema — *Psychological Human Cannonball*

Wes Unruh — *Stilt Walker/Meme Juggler*

Antero Alli — *ParaTheatricalist Extraordinaire*

P. Emerson Williams — *Necrofuturist Highwire Artist*

THE *Original* FALCON PRESS
TEMPE, ARIZONA, U.S.A.

International Standard Book Number: 978-1-935150-75-6

First Edition 2009

Address all inquiries to:
The Original Falcon Press
1753 East Broadway Road #101-277
Tempe, AZ 85282 U.S.A.
(or)
PO Box 3540
Silver Springs NV 89429 U.S.A.
website: http://www.originalfalcon.com
email: info@originalfalcon.com

THE POST OFFICE WALL

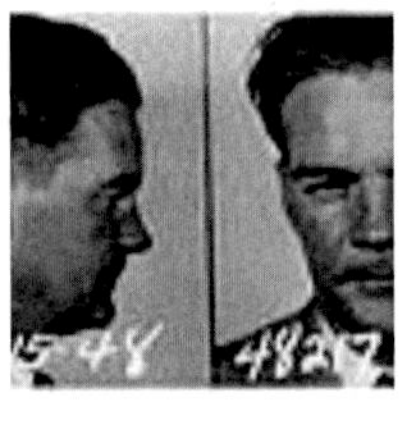

Christopher S. Hyatt, Ph.D.

www.drhyatt.net

Christopher Hyatt was trained in experimental and clinical psychology and practiced as a psychotherapist for many years. Today he is known as the world-famous author of books on self-transformation, psychology and Western magic.

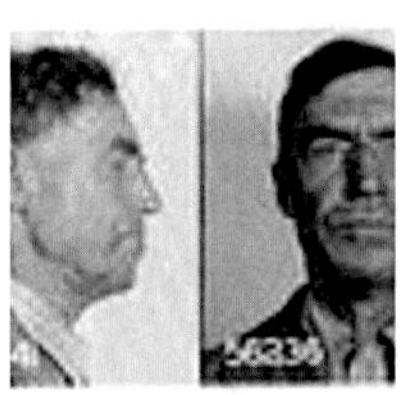

Joseph Matheny

jmatheny.wordpress.com

As it Is. Joseph Matheny is a hypermedium, cross-talk capable, fully open source, creative commons licensed human being. He infiltrates literature, TV, movies and the Internet for nefarious reasons. Good luck figuring out his affiliations. **So Be It.**

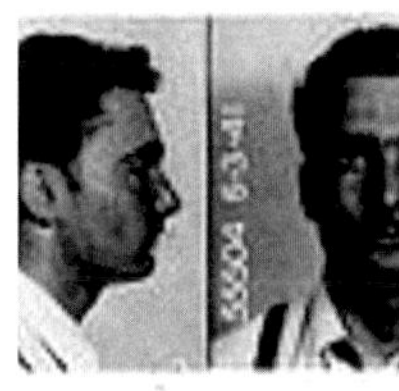

Nick Pell

www.blacksungazette.com

Nick Pell has been hard at the Hyatt Working for years. He has recently scraped the bottom of the barrel and is starting to rebuild himself into an actualized human being. He lives somewhere in the Pacific Northwest.

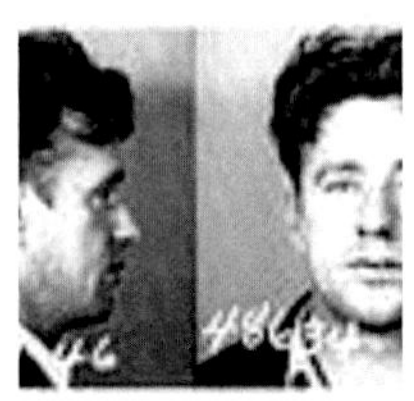

Calvin Iwema

www.bestmindforward.com

Calvin is a licensed psychological counselor, hypnotherapist, corporate consultant and the co-author of *Energized Hypnosis* (with Christopher S. Hyatt). He enjoys expanding perspectives, increasing personal power and assisting human monkeys in self-reprogramming.

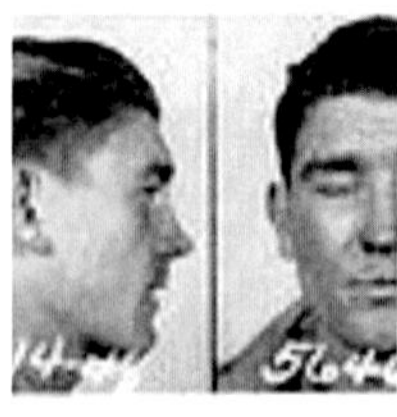

Wes Unruh

www.WesUnruh.com

Wes Unruh is an author who lives in upstate New York, spending his days plotting unspeakable acts designed to immanetize the eschaton. He is co-author, editor, and publisher of the non-fiction book The Art of Memetics.

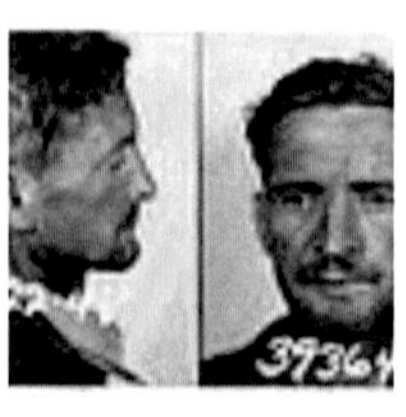

Antero Alli

www.paratheatrical.com

Antero Alli is an underground filmmaker and director of ParaTheatrical ReSearch who maintains a private astrological practice in his spare time. He is the author of *Angel Tech* and *A Modern Shaman's Guide to a Pregnant Universe* (with Christopher S. Hyatt) among many other works.

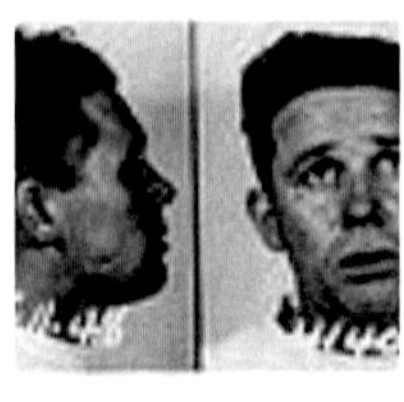

P. Emerson Williams

www.veilofthorns.com/blog

P. Emerson Williams is an artist/musician who works in a bat-cave built into a sweltering Florida bungalow. His discography spans over twenty years and five bands and his art has appeared in magazines and books from California to England, from Germany, Spain and Italy to Lithuania, Brazil and Colombia.

Watch www.alterati.com/gspot for an upcoming podcast roundtable with all the players from the center ring.

In memory of our friend and mentor, Dr. Christopher Hyatt, who is really hiding out on an island in the South Pacific but you didn't hear it from us.

Got it? —jmatheny

When in the height heaven was not named,
And the earth beneath did not yet bear a name,
And the primeval Apsu, who begat them,
And chaos, Tiamat, the mother of them both
Their waters were mingled together,
And no field was formed, no marsh was to be seen;
When of the gods none had been called into being,
And none bore a name, and no destinies were ordained;
Then were created the gods in the midst of heaven,
Lahmu and Lahamu were called into being...

I found myself
on the deck of a small sailboat
in the middle of the Pacific.
I looked at the sky
filled with stars
and realized that I was a simple perceiver.
At that moment I became
the ultimate egoist.
— C.S. Hyatt

Brand EII? — jmatheny

My Report

Joseph Matheny

Dear Doc,

I did it. I have the boat. (See *Black Book III: Galt's Ark, Parts 1 & 2*) Now I have to find someone else to co-pilot it with me, damn you, but I have the boat. We have named her, ***The Tiamat***. What we will do with it…well, you know, even writing it secretly in my journal, to a friend who has passed on, feels dangerous. Maybe it's time to think of dead fish.

Anyway, the plan is to have her sail out of Marina Del Rey, CA and to secure a second vessel, which will sail out of an east coast port. Maybe somewhere in Florida, Nantucket or Long Island. I think I will name the second one, ***Qingu***. We eventually plan to have 5–10 boats in a fleet, positioned in major ports around the world.

The Tiamat docked in Nantucket

So, now that I have completed this task, I have a question for you: How does it feel to have pulled off a stunt that to date has only been successfully completed by a handful of operatives that have gone before you? (Andy Kaufman, Alan Abel, Jim Morrison, to name a few). I would think that you gloated for a day and then swiftly got on to executing your parts of Projekt Apokalypse. I have been receiving the anonymous updates and completion forms at the P.O. Box 661252 at the 90066 LA drop point. I must say, I was a little shocked at the first contact, and for a brief second, I felt a twinge of hurt that you were sending them anonymously, with no greeting or fond farewells, but then I remembered that was never how we communicated anyway, so it passed a nanosecond later. </whiny little bitch mode>

Oh, yeah. I also got the ring that you sent via courier. Thanks. (See The Chromokids: *Black Book III, Galt's Ark, Part 1.*)

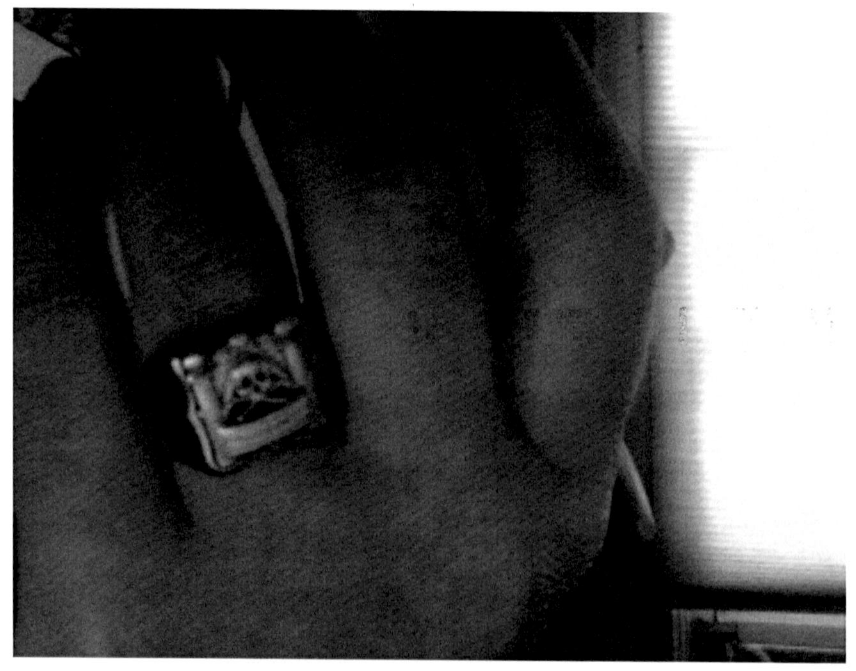

One ring to bind them...

Now to the rest of the news.

We have lost a few more operatives to the attrition of "life as we know it" which is shocking, since they all had exposure to the "SHIVA" code. I am perplexed as to why they chose to continue to adhere to a contract that they had never signed, but I guess it's "each to their own" and so I move forward with a smaller, but definitely more elegant and efficient team. I guess one side of the coin says, "All things happen for a reason" (while the other still says, "This shit is all random"). You were one of the few people I knew…er, people I know… who can consistently flip the coin and have it land on its edge. I won't bother to give you the list of the recently fallen, because I'm sure you're monitoring the frequencies at the island base.

As you will see by this crytpo-report, I have camouflaged the troops as a psycho-circvs. You know me, coming from a circus family and all, it was inevitable that I return to my roots. I think that this gives us the perfect cover to arrive in a designated geographic area in the dead of night and to extract from said area in the same manner. We tested it out in a few areas using the "Y" variant (citizen-y.com) with the standard subdirectory for administrative reports, with the level 64 username/password combo. Also, the report in this document can be decoded using the PGP Public key that is in the subdirectory below the report directory, named according to the defcon 2 level naming conventions. I am, of course, assuming you took your codebook with you.

Also, the 4P2 experiment gave us some very interesting results. However, it still leaves our minor disagreement unresolved. I am speaking, of course, of the 10% versus 2% debate. The 4P2.org results was a 50/50 split between people who wanted to join and learn to be serial killers and 50% people who wanted to kill us. (The latter were, of course, all from the hysterical conspiracy dupe camp.) This does not speak well of the human condition.

The only other things I have to report at this time is that the project to infiltrate and infect Hollywood is moving along smoothly and so far we've only had a few major run-ins with the Scientologists. Once you peel back the layers of plastic and tinsel in this town, you, of course, find… Also, there is a site called the New EII. (neweii.com). Do you have anything to do with this? I am in communication with a "Phage

Darkfyre" who claims to be the outer-head of this org. Maybe you're having some fun playing me? If it is you I hope you're enjoying it.

I will send this message by the normal means, encrypted with the usual algorithm, and hidden in the most obvious places. Then I will go fishing and wait for your reply.

Guns and Dope my friend,
-JM
Venice California
July 12, 2009

Remember my Dear Buddha:
A criminal is simply a person
who has disobeyed someone
of greater power.
— C.S. Hyatt

DOCTOR HYATT IS BORING

by Christopher S. Hyatt, Ph.D.

Dear Dr. Hyatt:

You are a bore. Your program was too hard, took too much time, so I have joined a group (the Mother Goddess) and feel a lot better about myself. Your work led to boredom and now I feel excited again and that is good. Doing those exercises over and over again, and following your complete program took about eight hours a week. Now that I have more time I feel better and am learning a lot more about things. No doubt a number of people have realized the same thing about your Self Magic. I think you need to try something different yourself, maybe you wouldn't be so boring.

Dr. Hyatt says:

Emotions are promiscuous; so are thoughts and tensions. They will sleep with anyone who is willing to pay. ::::::::: In these instances the currency is attention.::;:::::: If you pay these whores of the spirit too much they will possess you—they will turn into beliefs, habits and other horrors. I often ask students "what would you be without your memory?" The answers I get often amaze me. Some are outright insane, such as "I wouldn't know how to skate or play basketball." Now these answers are coming from people who are possessed—possessed by their identity as sufferers, losers in life, addicts of all kinds. They live in a perpetual pity party…yet they refuse to let go. Whatever comes up in their lives they bring their whole history with them…and each piece of their precious little self is taking a free ride on the present and their possible futures. They want to know—NO—they **demand** to know—the outcome of their life. They bury each and every encounter of the dynamic flow of pulsating cells and particles into their image patterns and worse, those of their caretakers. They force fit everything into their memories—allowing nothing to escape. They need a perpetual party, a never-ending fix to survive.

Many of these people are sensory-tonic handicapped which, put in simple language means that they don't know what is going on. They have thoughts, emotions etc. but they never dig deep enough… And if and when they do, what they find is…… Nothing……and that scares them to death. Yes there is Nothing there. After their beloved enemies (often parents) have died there is Nothing there. When they have stopped reacting like the people they have hated, dropped their traumas and the novels they have written for themselves, there is Nothing there……and they are scared to death. There is no salvation, their Gods have been turned into the hired help, and they are alone for the first time. Faced with the possibility of inner peace, happiness and excitement, they run away… So much for bondage…… And guess what Boredom is: it is the first deep sign you are getting close…very close… :::::::::::::::::: So run now—before it is too late and you can't go back. Run—run—run!!

Panic! — P. Emerson Williams

Now, look to the cage in the center ring as Nick Pell, Dogma Tamer, places his head in the mouth of a roaring belief!

Tantra Motherfucker: The Importance of Christopher Hyatt

I remember the days when I first got into this non-sense. I'm no longer as naive as I once was. The wonderful neo-Salad Days of college when we all thought The Invisibles was going to "emerge" at any given second. People spoke very seriously about the importance of The Great Beast. Everyone did so many fucking drugs that we really believed that Earth was a giant monster waiting to eat us, or that "reality isn't what it seems." As it turns out, The Invisibles are cool but chock full of bullshit, Thelema is just as thought-killing as any other religion, and reality is pretty much exactly what it seems. Had I just listened to a bellicose drunk name of Alan Miller aka Dr. Christopher Hyatt I could have saved myself a lot of embarrassing conversations.

Dr. Hyatt was a guru, albeit the kind of guru that you could become co-equal with…if you could navigate his Byzantine, "bury the dog deeper" system of Tantra derived from Aleister Crowley by way of Israel Regardie, Dr. Wilhelm Reich, the Gurdjieff work, and the man's own collaborations with contemporary dogma busters Dr. Timothy Leary, Antero Alli, and, of course, the Laughing Buddha of the psychedelic generation, Robert Anton Wilson. Many negative things can be said of Dr. Hyatt, and those of us emotionally and (dare I say it?) spiritually attached to him will likely not disagree. But all of this misses the most obvious and important truth. The keys to enlightenment can be pulled out of twenty or so pages of his seminal work, *Undoing Yourself With Energized Meditation and Other Devices* (Falcon Press).

I've heard a lot of whining and moaning from lily-livered simpletons who bemoan there being "only twenty or so pages of really useful stuff." In the first place, I think this is a mischaracterization. There is a treasure trove of material in the rest of the book, which is not merely a book. It is a talisman designed to destroy the safe little temple of your ego and perhaps build something useful in its place. If you doubt me, read the book again. You should be able to rock it out in about an hour or two if you've read it before, and the text is much deeper than it appears to be upon repeated readings.

Throughout the book Hyatt alternately lambastes and cajoles the ego of the reader. This has a number of simultaneous effects. Attacks on the ego result in the ego defending itself, shoring itself up, and asserting to itself very firmly that "Oh, he can't possibly be talking about me" or perhaps even "What an asshole." On the other hand, the flattery of the ego results in defenses getting dropped and the ego affirms loudly "Of course, I am one of the enlightened elites of which the good doctor speaks!" The combined effect of the two techniques is perhaps the most important. One of the major tasks that the neophyte student of Tantra must undertake is destroying their dualistic thinking. Either/or is a terribly limited way of thinking, and the rubric of either/or/both/neither/some/none/all/always/never/ sometimes/etc. is a much more flexible way of thinking. The alternating assault on the ego utilize the best traditions of Taoist meditation and Western psychology. For a very simple way to experience the effect quickly meditate on pairs of opposites. Black/white. Hate/love. Etc. Do this for a week.

However, unlike the simpleton offended by the supposed "filler" material in *Undoing,* Dr. Hyatt never allowed his reason to suffer from option paralysis. In an interview with S. Jason Black, Dr. Hyatt takes exception to Mr. Black's assertion that Ayn Rand's philosophy is like *The Book of the Law* by saying "Well, there's a difference, Ayn Rand was a real thinker, *The Book of the Law* is a bunch of bullshit." My objections to the bizarre capitalist cult of Ayn Rand aside, Dr. Hyatt doesn't say *The Book of the Law* might be bullshit. He doesn't say it seems like bullshit. He doesn't say parts of it are bullshit. He says it's a bunch of bullshit. Because for Christopher Hyatt, even in a world of many-layered truth some truths are eternal. One of those truths is that religion, no matter what name it goes by, is the death of human thought, the oppressor of the human spirit, and the first thing that must be defeated for humanity to become liberated from its sordid past. This is a truth that Dr. Hyatt never pulled punches on. He fought the fight against religion the best way he knew how, without ever hiding behind the worst elements of Taoism (religion!) cloaked under the guise of "fuzzy logic" or any other bullshit that people talk about a lot but don't understand.

There have been and will continue to be many attacks on the life and person of Dr. Christopher Hyatt. And why wouldn't there be, now that he has abandoned his body to continue his research in the Western Lands? His enemies are largely the biggest collection of psychic weaklings around, clinging to their religion, and their rituals, and their idols. Now that he isn't there to respond to their slurs (as if the Good Doctor would ever deign to respond to such cripples) every mediocre hack with a keyboard will come out of the woodwork, proclaiming the shortcomings of the man, and his life. As if that has anything to do with his life's work. There are any number of reasons to impugn the personality of Christopher Hyatt, and those of who have devoted ourselves to continuing his life's work on this plane of existence are fully aware of them—perhaps more so than the phony mystics, psychedelic posers, and ersatz priests who have made it their job to try and sodomize the man's corpse before the body was cold. Whenever you hear some overgrown child hemming and hawing about the man's various and sundry shortcomings, either close your ears or ball your fist, depending on thy will.

Having defended Dr. Hyatt, it seems necessary to say why he needs defending. The most obvious reasons have been stated above. But what about the man's work is so important that people such as myself, who are notorious non-joiners and non-followers, have dedicated their lives to continuing his work? It seems worth pointing out that while what I will, for simplicities sake, and with apologies to G.I. Gurdjieff, refer to as the Hyatt Working is difficult, arduous, and long, it is also not something that (I hope) any of us undertake out of a sense of obligation. Indeed, one mark of what Dr. Hyatt called an Extreme Individual is that they are dissatisfied with conditioned life and couldn't imagine living their life any way but punching and kicking their way out of the shell built around them by history, society, family, friends, and lovers.

We do the work because we couldn't live with ourselves otherwise.

But what is the Hyatt Working? Everyone reading this has likely at least read *Undoing* or *The Psychopath's Bible* (Falcon Press). Between the two of those, you have a pretty clear picture of what the work is, why we do it, and what ends we hope to accomplish.

First and foremost, the Hyatt Working is about self-creation. It is about being exactly who the fuck we want to be without interference by the laws of invisible sky monsters or cloying psychic weaklings.

The occult community, being largely a bunch of weak-willed simpletons, superstitious scaredy cats, crypto-religionists, and straight up raving lunatics, is full of these people. They are just like their straight counterparts save for their aesthetic choice of ancient deities, bad haircuts, and sinfully ugly clothing. The Hyatt Working community could not be more different. Hyatt was, first and foremost, a blue collar son-of-a-bitch and you can see this in the people who follow him. We are—to a man—completely uninterested in following social convention and wish to chart our own path through the world. In doing so we make lots of enemies, powerful and otherwise. Because few things are more offensive to the world at large than a man who does not give a solitary, single fuck. Self-creation ultimately means ending your need for validation from others and seeking only the validation which matters—the validation that comes from within. Christopher Hyatt understood this better than any other radical psychologist of his generation. But how does one get there?

That is where the bulk of our praxis comes from. First, one must eliminate the Reichian "blockages" put in place by the traumatic process of socialization. In substance this means dutifully committing to the work outlined in *Undoing*. One fairly obvious proof that Dr. Hyatt was onto something is his understanding that the physical body is the first thing that must be broken down and rebuilt. He did not start with lofty theory or puerile religion. He started with the science of destroying bodily tensions to create a firm basis for re-creating the self in thy own image. Nowhere in Hyatt will you find anything that wasn't confirmed by his own experience and experiments. Anyone who doesn't notice physical changes, biochemical changes, and neurological changes simply isn't conducting the experiments properly. Get rid of the props, get rid of the noise, break your muscles, and then shut your mouth for a change.

Following liberating the body from deeply stored muscle tension begins the process of de-socialization. Another thing that the doctor understood that those who seek the quick, easy, religious path towards enlightenment do not is that the process of socialization is traumatic and enslaving. This is not the trauma that gets whined and moaned about every day on *Oprah*. This is the unavoidable trauma of growing up in a society with dogma pushers and conformity cops on all sides pushing, prodding, pulling, picking apart your wild child psyche and forcing it not into an Apollonian, mature version of itself, but rather into the best little cog in the machine that they think you should be. De-socialization is the modern, scientific way of breaking taboo, of breaking state, of smashing the superego others built for you to create your own.

In a world where we are circumscribed by factors beyond our control, we can at least be free in our own minds and bodies. Dr. Hyatt knew this. He didn't cry about the world he found himself in. He didn't lay down in the middle of the road, crouched into the fetal position, allowing himself to be the victim of circumstance. Dr. Hyatt is the Bukowski of Yoga, a modern day Bodhidharma who found the path out of the darkness and brought back a map for anyone clever enough to know how to read it. And he never once lied about just how hard it is to pull yourself up from a grave the world buried you in. You dismiss him as only a belligerent crank at your own peril.

Goodbye, Dr. Hyatt. See you in the Western Lands.

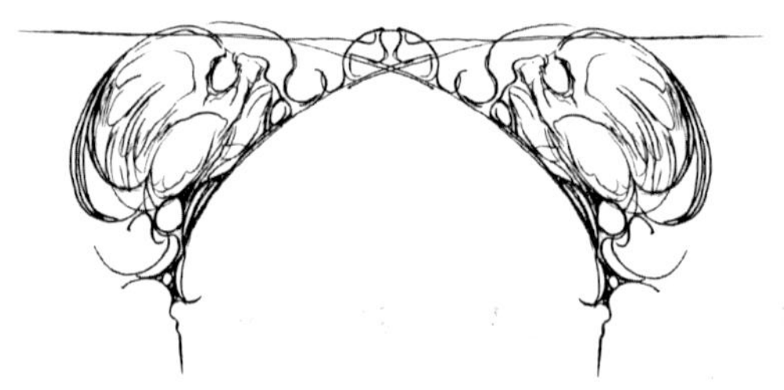

Inner Flight — P. Emerson Williams

INTEGRITY

by Christopher S. Hyatt, Ph.D.

Integrity and self-respect are intimately related… Self-respect and integrity are similar to a bank account with deposits and withdrawals, though unlike a bank account integrity and self-respect can have a negative balance…

In man there are strong instincts and one is to have more, to have everything…as much as possible… However, this instinct is balanced (in theory) by a desire for self-respect. So a man of integrity will be willing to pay for his vices, desires and needs… If a man has such a desire to have self-respect and doesn't pay he loses integrity, he begins to feel self-hate, he begins to feel unworthy, like he is not a human, not a person , he feels like a fraud… However, paying means giving something up, and most humans do not like to give anything up…

A man searching for self-respect must finally admit that to have integrity he must forgo certain other desires. He must give up certain pleasures which violates his sense of self-worth… His internal strength is a result of giving up certain things and accepting the discomfort without complaining. Why? He is not giving up a pleasure for someone else, or for some external morality, but he is giving something up for *himself.* Hence to complain about giving something up for his integrity is, in a sense, a complaint against himself…a complaint against his desire for self respect…

Unlike most things in life, integrity and self-respect is a "dutch treat": each man must pay the price for himself; no one can pay the price for him lest he has no integrity. Hence integrity is born from the man himself; it is his own most primal concern…and he knows that having integrity and self-respect can at times be very costly…so each man must decide what prices he is willing to pay…

The refusal to pay the price coupled with the desire for self-respect can weaken a man to a point of shame and self-disgust. His refusal, together with his desire for self-respect, eat away at him, reducing him in his own eyes to a worthless slug…

So in the end integrity becomes a choice and it must be a reasonable internal choice, not one based on external shoulds… Integrity is a man's own concern. In the end it is only he who knows if he has won the battle to be a man…

Ring, Fire, Immolation — P. Emerson Williams

And now, direct your eyes upward for Calvin Iwema — Psychological Human Cannonball

The Success Robot Experiment

If you want to change your life, get busy and do it…
Being mean to yourself is the habit of slaves, so just drop it……
…stop the self talk and do something.
— From *Black Book II: Extreme: The Twisted Man*

The Success Robot Experiment will increase your awareness and help you to accomplish more in your life. It contains an awareness component and a behavior component. Remember that real results and understanding only come from actually doing the experiment, not from reading. You will be best served if you get a journal and write down your thoughts and progress.

Pick an area of your life that you want to change, something that you want to accomplish. This might be something in your life that you are procrastinating about, a new skill you want to develop or goal you want to reach. Think about all the things you are capable of accomplishing. You might look to the Despair Coefficient Test to find something.

Imagine that you acquired a robot that looked exactly like you. Think along the lines of Data from *Star Trek* or Bishop from the movie *Aliens*. You could program it to do the things you want to do. It would dominate. It would be wildly successful, because it would not have the limitations a human has.

Humans, unlike robots, have the unique ability to know what they need to do and not do it. Even when it is in their very best interest, humans find ways to not do things. There is no shortage of information on losing weight, saving and investing money, the long-term effects of certain habits and so forth, yet the percentage of humans who are overweight, die broke or from lung cancer and never read another book after high school are staggering.

The basic reason for this due to the way we develop and the way we use our brains and nervous systems for self-preservation. Our emotions end up being tied to concepts, such as "right and wrong", "good and "evil, " etc. We believe in these concepts when we are very young because we are told to and also because of the consequences of disobedience. Oftentimes these concepts exist only to serve other people. Even if we come to understand differently and see past this game, our nervous system still operates on auto-pilot and "keeps us in line" though our emotions, which can be ***very*** powerful (just watch someone experience a panic attack.) If you want to read more about this in detail, read *Energized Hypnosis: A Non-Book for Self Change* (Falcon Press).

The Success Robot Experiment goes like this:

1) Pick a goal you would like to reach. Could be changing a habit, losing weight, getting in shape, completing school, etc. Write your goal down.

2) Determine the steps and necessary behaviors. You need a solid plan that will take you to your goal. If you aren't sure, do the research and get help. Your plan should have specific behaviors with a time-line. Write this plan down.

3) Think about how you will feel engaging in those behaviors. Think about where you might normally lose interest, feel bad in some way, or quit. Where are those areas for you in terms of the goal you picked? Where do you get hung up? What happens internally? What do you say to yourself about yourself? Write these things down.

4) Think about how the Success Robot is different from you in terms of #3. Does the robot get stuck where you do? No. Does the robot treat itself poorly and judge itself? No. Really meditate on this, think about all the implications of the differences between the Success Robot and you. Write down your thoughts.

5) Pretend you are the robot, and engage in the behaviors, just as the robot would: This is the key. Robots follow their programs without thinking about them or talking about them or talking about how they feel about them. Your job is to follow the plan (program) you determined above until you reach your goal. Your emotions and anxieties may flare up…plan on it.

engage in your plan and move toward your goal as if you were the success robot.

6) Come up with a way to keep this front-of-mind. Develop a ritual for remembering and reminding yourself. Re-read your journal. Read this article or your plan and journal every morning when you wake up and every evening before you go to sleep.

7) Keep going. Develop persistence. Did the *Terminator* quit? No. Never.

Accelerating….

Think on these questions and ideas. Meditate on them. Write down the implications of them, and your thoughts in your journal.

If you struggle, hesitate or feel bad/wrong during this experiment, ask yourself "Why would one want to carry the past into the future and repeat their limitations and suffering?" "Who does my being limited serve?" Write down these answers in your journal.

Self-enhancing is a supreme value. Is there any reason not to be the success robot?

Doing what works and succeeding might *feel* like it's self-diminishing and dangerous. This is the steering mechanism of the robot. Do you want to serve the feelings, which are from the past and were learned at a young age when you didn't know any better and couldn't defend yourself? Or do you want to get what you want?

Do you really want to serve the feelings, which will strengthen the erroneous beliefs they imply? Or do you want to find out what you are really capable of and live powerfully?

Do you want to be a good little boy/girl and agree with mommy/daddy/authority? Or are you smart enough and independent enough to decide what is good for you?

Should I be spending more energy on self-enhancing things than I am?

-- -- -- -- -- -- --

As you follow through with the experiment, some things might happen. You will either reach your goal or figure out a more suitable one. You will learn much about yourself, your programming and the process of real change. You will learn much about your emotions, the information that they provide and how they are connected to your original programming. You might find out a lot about any chronic anxieties and tensions that you have ignored, both physically and psychologically.

You may also find that you are not your emotions, and that your emotions do not prove the beliefs and concepts instilled from your original programming. As you free yourself from the emotions generated by your original programming (guilt, anxiety, fear, shame) you will be able to accomplish more and truly become who you are.

If you want a guarantee, buy a toaster.
— Clint Eastwood

BECOME WHO YOU ARE—
THERE ARE NO GUARANTEES

WORTHLESSNESS

by Christopher S. Hyatt, Ph.D.

Worthlessness: the state of being useless, of no value. In psychology, the feeling and/or thought that one is of little or no value.

If there is a fundamental, pervasive and total assumption that one is worthless, no matter what is accomplished or how one is viewed by others, the feeling remains…as well as an array of self-destructive behavior.

The thought and feeling of worthlessness demands a world-view and lifestyle consistent with the assumption.

A person in this condition demands that the world treat him in such a way that is consistent with his assumption. At the same time the person demands complete and absolute unconditional acceptance. Although this appears contradictory on the surface, it is not.

The assumption of worthlessness is extremely painful, and as such the person demands relief from the pain. Since utter worthlessness is a an over-generalization, it is psychologically correct that the only cure is absolute, unconditional acceptance—another over-generalization. This need is never presented as a "request" but always is presented as a demand which, if not met, is followed by depression and aggression.

The concept "worthlessness" is developmentally advanced. In no case would a person without an advanced conceptual ability label this pervasive feeling as such.

Initially what a person feels is pain, and only after numerous painful experiences is a label such as worthlessness—or the feeling of worthlessness—applied to similar painful experiences.

Worthlessness is also a value judgment. Children learn labels from adults. Thus, a child who is condemned will accept the labels adults place on him.

The feeling of worthlessness has no neurological or biological basis. It does have a *conceptual* basis as explained above.

Worthlessness is a value judgment made by people who are making evaluations based on their own desires, and needs.

A scientist may say that a chemical is worthless in treating a certain disease. The use of the term is contextual and is limited to a set of specific facts. Taken out of the specific context the term becomes a value judgment—most often based on the labeler's values and needs.

Fortaert — P. Emerson Williams

And now, working without a net, in the center ring: Wes Unruh — Stilt Walker/Meme Juggler

Yes, you CAN take over the world!

Take stock of your position in life—is there a way for you to advance, to grow in power where you are now? If not, quit. Leave it all behind. Take whatever equipment you can carry and head for somewhere else.

All of life's problems are solved by movement. Any resistance you meet along the way can be overcome so long as you recognize what kind of resistance with which you're being confronted. To take control of someone's will, you must present them with a compelling movement they can take which will unlock a benefit you present.

There are three types of individuals who stand in your way. Skeptics, who'll always be uncertain about the benefit you are touting; reactors, who resist because they sense your underlying intentions; and reluctants, who are slowly turning to stone on their own and who wouldn't want to change no matter what you or anyone else offers.

Institutional structures are surprisingly easy targets for the motivated psychopath, because they're filled with redundancies, absurdities, and entropic points of exploitable inertia. Rising through the ranks of any given institution is purely a matter of social manipulation, NOT experience, and certainly NOT by being a TEAM PLAYER. If you fit in too well, you'll never move up the institutional pyramid.

You must start by exploring the nature of the institution carefully. Create a network map of the institution you want to bend to your will, and identify both the core network that runs things and the peripheral network that kow-tows to the demands of the core network.

Once you've identified all the key players in the core network, pay close attention to the different language choices those in the core network you wish to infiltrate use as opposed to those in the periphery that have no power. Mimic that language deliberately. It will feel forced, but only to you, and that feeling will quickly fade. Soon you'll sound like a member of the core network and that subliminal effect will have the 'team players' running around doing your bidding EVEN IF YOU MAKE LESS MONEY THAN THEY DO.

Any time you meet with resistance, immediately seek a way of structuring a change in your relationship with that person. Sidestep resistance by creating a positive vision of their future that they can only achieve by following your specific suggestions. Minimize your requests at first, and depersonalize the interactions, so you are redefining the relationship you have with that resisting individual.

Get them to say yes to something, anything, first, before you make your real request. Even better, give them something. If you are in a corporate environment that has a break room with vending machines, this becomes absurdly easy. Go buy yourself two sodas and bring them by your target's desk—casually say the machine spit out an extra soda, and give it to them. Don't even give them an opportunity to say no, just put it on their desk.

Then, two or three hours later, make your request in such a way as to provide them with upwardly scalable responses—don't ask for a specific thing, ask for general assistance where your target can choose their level of response—often they will go above and beyond what you expect, especially if they've drunk the soda, or eaten the candy, or otherwise accepted the gift you'd left them hours earlier.

When you make a request, be sure to use the word 'Because' in the request. You don't even need to give a real reason, ending the sentence with the word 'Because' is ammunition enough to work your mind control. Injecting desired behavior changes into an institutional body means mimicking all the acceptable group behavior long enough that you've been accepted by the core network, then bending those members of the periphery network to your will.

Modulate the way you ask these 'team players' to do something—asking directly may work on the reluctant ones who need a direct shock to motivate them into action, but those who react oppositionally to a direct request are often easier to motivate through insinuation… 'It sure would be good if someone did X' is an easier sell to these types than 'I need you to do X'—and with the skeptics out there, you'll find that you must build up over time a relationship based around gifting them and getting them to say yes to questions long before you begin really manipulating them directly.

Persuasion is both an art-form and a science, and there are thousands of books written on the subject, a few even worth reading. This is in no way a complete course in manipulation, read the rest of the *Black*

Books and *The Psychopath's Bible* closely enough and you'll get a crash course in manipulation. Instead this piece is intended to help you step out of your powerless rut.

Forget about strategies for getting ahead in business, or spending time getting a post-graduate degree. If you really want to master your time and space, first you must quit whatever piss-poor job you're doing now to make ends meet.

You can take control of any given situation in a matter of minutes with the right stimulus—and a competent manipulator can quickly rise through the social structure of any institution by keeping a few basic techniques for dealing with resistance.

Nearly all institutions, both public and private, are essentially pyramidal in structure, while the individuals embedded within those institutions are part of a larger social body which is primarily constructed out of circles that move in waves between institutions. Rising up the pyramid means finding new social circles to surf—and it doesn't matter how competent you may or may not be at your occupation so long as the social circle you want to manipulate accepts you as part of itself.

When you quit whatever bullshit you've been doing to just get by, and start using others around you to promote your own interests, you're well on your way to realizing your full potential. You're also going to have some really fucked up experiences, mainly because you'll have freed up enough time for those experiences. It's not going to be easy, but it sure as fuck won't be boring.

Untitled — P. Emerson Williams

Learn to expend yourself on the right things.
If you do, you will never feel unhappy.
— Christopher S. Hyatt, Ph.D.

FULFILLMENT

by Christopher S. Hyatt, Ph.D.

In dividing those things which men assert to provide fulfillment we can break them into three groups:

things—money—power to move
people—friends, family, honors, rank
god, loved by and loving god, angels, spiritual quests…
Rarely do you hear a man say "I am fulfillment."

Is a man only of value if he is the subject of some object?

If I lived on a desert isle alone would I be of no value because there was no one to shower my gifts upon?

How does the idea of value come under the authority of "the other"? and who would invent a medal for those whose efforts and nature shower the world with their glory? Those in need of water… those who want to build a dam…

I want to look like an honorable man, a heroic man, hence I make up riddles which sooth the spirits of little men…

The arrow was painful. Can it not be painful without your comparing it to something, something even as common as childbirth?

If all there is is our physiology, then we better learn to remain healthy, avoid pain, and bask in the sun when it shines…

Why do I want to be more? Because I am unhealthy, and use weakness to survive…

I am neither smart enough, strong enough nor prominent enough to save myself—let alone promote myself—so, like a woman, I use deception to gain the little comfort and moments of triumph that can only come from being a regular at a bar for pensioners…

I loathe any form of resistance to my desires and if I must act, I put myself out to satisfy myself. I gain more from the bragging of my struggles than the object which I desired to begin with…

We have invented all sorts of conveniences to resist the fact that we are factual and are being lived by a series of secret bacteria whose death means our own. They care little for what we think of ourselves or what we own, or what we want… All they care about is simply going on… Simply study the various forms of getting rid of the corpse, of how we can go on so easily…and how we hurry to have it done with…everyone has a turn with the shovel… The sooner we forget the quicker we can get on with it… Life must go on…and it does and it doesn't care what body it occupies…

The man is proud. He never gets caught in his petty crimes against mankind and god, he got his little house, his aging wife and 4 grand-children to show for it… Proud is he, much like the prison guard who is protecting society against those who got caught.

In punishment the executioner learns more than the victim…it is possible.

To stay alive we have given up life…

How a little tick in the evening can make us forget the pleasures of the day…

Less than 10% of the race is born healthy and thus cheerful and happy… The rest work at it at worst or hope for it at best, thus making the world go round… Most people live a life of almost. The almost get the carrot in front of their nose…

Where there is pleasure much pain will soon follow. The price of great pleasure is often greater pain…

People take risky chances for a fictitious payoff. And this is the key: anything but boredom…even pain…

Often in the search of a specific goal, we find everything but what we were looking for. The secret is to learn and enjoy what you did find…

Most people on vacation believe that the only way they know they were on vacation is to exhaust themselves and return home sick…

Now marvel as the mighty Antero Alli lifts a pallet of heavy superstitions over his head and tosses them like a rag doll!

Paratheatre Manifesto

Part One: Culture, Paratheatre and the Emotional Plague

culture

We tend to think of "culture" as a thing and also a very big thing; hence, the smaller subcultures, microcultures, macrocultures. Culture expresses a dynamic process, not a thing, that manifests itself in similar ways regardless of size. Individuals can participate in a culture, as can couples, groups, "subcultures" and entire sectors of any given society. The phenomena of culture is also romanticized, mythologized and stratified into hierarchical spectrums between high and low culture. This thing called "culture" also arouses powerful investments of status, propriety and pride from those who identify with what they call their culture.

According to Dr. Christopher S. Hyatt's anthropological theories, the impersonal (and unsentimental) basis of all human culture expresses no more and no less than genes interacting with geography. This mutual feeding process—the earth feeds us, we feed the earth—bonds human DNA with its immediate womb environment. We settle somewhere, figure out how to survive and develop relationships inside the power fields of the bioregion sustaining us. Culture is not something we "create" as much as participate in, augment, diminish, corrupt, subvert, develop with and otherwise act on and be acted upon by.

Over time—decades, centuries, ages—this genes/geography interaction slowly crystallizes into symbols, languages, and artifacts that encode, encrypt and transmit its characteristics as a distinct cultural identity. Cultures developing in mountainous regions differ from cultures stimulated along oceanic shorelines or in deserts or lush valleys or forests. Each unique bioregion influences its people in specific ways that inform their religions, art, mythologies, commerce, education, community and family life. The power and presence of the planet acts on people, just as the power and presence of people act on the planet. Any human culture achieves longevity by the success of its sustaining rituals and theatre is one of these rituals. The question this manifesto addresses and attempts to answer is: how can the sustaining ritual of theatre be renewed and sustained when it loses vitality and dies?

paratheatre

As with any sustaining ritual, the nature and purpose of theatre must evolve and change over time to meet the emergent needs of its originating culture. Like a snake shedding old skin, any culture grows by outgrowing itself. Any theatre that does not outgrow itself ceases to function as a vital sustaining ritual. Dead theatre results. For theatre to remain vital, a kind of "paratheatre" must be developed and utilized to explore, nurture and challenge the performer's innermost primordial interactions between his/her own vertical sources (via the DNA/ Central Nervous System/Body feedback loop) and the immediate womb environment of the existing cultural zeitgeist.

Historically this dialogue has been achieved by various esoteric schools utilizing various methods of sense-deprivation (withdrawal of identification from external stimuli) towards realignment with vertical sources. Monastic orders, various Tantric and Vedic yogas, cosmologies and meditation practices have met this spiritual task towards the promise of salvation and/or enlightenment. Add to this, the numerous systems of psychotherapy and mysticism exploring this same process in the dialogue between Ego and the Unconscious through such examples as Carl Jung's Individuation, Dada Bhagwan's Self-realization, Dr. Abraham Mazlow's Self-Actualization, G.I. Gurdjieff's Self-Work and so forth.

However, rarely have any of these methods ever been used for the purpose of regenerating the sustaining ritual of theatre, its originating culture and/or the culture of the society at large. One strident exception to all of this arrived with the compelling work of the late visionary of the theatre, Jerzy Grotowski (Aug. 11, 1933–Jan. 14, 1999). Grotowski coined the term 'paratheatre' to address a stage of work his group was doing between 1969 and 1977 in Poland. It should also be known that Grotowski claimed no actual 'legacy of paratheatre' due, in part, to the transmutations his work underwent over three decades (and beyond his death at the Workcenter of Jerzy Grotowski and

Thomas Richards in Pontedera, Italy) and also to his abhorrence and avoidance of canonization.

With respect to Grotowski's seminal work and the current and future work of his protégés in Pontedera, the term "paratheatre" will be used hereafter to reflect my ongoing paratheatrical research here in Berkeley California USA since 1977. Generally speaking, I refer to paratheatre as any private, non-performance oriented process of group ritual dynamics involving rigorous physical and vocal techniques for accessing, embodying and expressing the internal landscape. Without an audience the focus shifts away from the external pressures to perform or play for an audience and towards the self-created pressures of executing songs and ritual actions with enough commitment, skill and talent to transform the instrument of the actor.

VERTICALITY and ASOCIAL INTENT

It can be healthy and natural for any group to meet, develop rapport and do things together to form bonds as a community-building social event. However if these same social bonds inhibit or frustrate the expression of true feelings and responses and/or in any way block our access to the internal landscape then, no paratheatre can result. When a group becomes preoccupied with the masks and games played to meet our social needs—for friendship, courtship, belonging, approval, security, status and so forth—we are diverted away from verticality, from those vital and asocial sources of energy and information flowing from above, within and below.

With verticality the point is not to renounce part of our nature; all should retain its natural place: the body, the heart, the head, something that is "under our feet" and something that is "over the head." All like a vertical line, and this verticality should be held taut between organicity and the awareness. Awareness means the consciousness which is not linked to language (the machine for thinking), but to Presence.

— Jerzy Grotowski

One purpose of paratheatre is to increase the force of commitment to this verticality towards the transmission of its presence to the horizontal realms of the world. Paratheatre training must challenge and nurture an ongoing commitment to and dependence on vertical sources. To implement this shift from external to internal dependence, a certain asocial intent must be applied within the actual working climate where paratheatre occurs. Without this shift from the social to the asocial, the "default" conditioning of our local culture's socialization 'programs' tends to dominate the tone of all self-work and interpersonal interaction. When such a tone dominates, the quality of work suffers from social clichés and conditioned reactions, rather than being revitalized by the wellsprings of our most authentic, spontaneous responses.

Any asocial climate naturally frustrates social needs for seeking acceptance, approval, status, courting and flirting, belonging, and other needs for emotional and social support. An asocial intent and climate can temporarily suspend these external motivations by replacing them with a deepening internal dependence on our vertical sources for support. The initial stages of this shift necessitate a certain non-responsibility to others. Rather than depend on the audience and other performers for support and energy, we source ourselves. We learn to access what Carl Jung calls "the archetype of The Self."

The Self is a quantity that is supra ordinate to the conscious ego. It embraces not only the conscious but also the unconscious psyche, and is therefore, so to speak, a personality which we also are. The Self is not only the centre but also the whole circumference which embraces both conscious and unconscious; it is the centre of this totality, just as the ego is the center of consciousness.

— Carl Jung, *Two Essays on Analytical Psychology*

In other words, the individual Ego emerges from the Self—the Self does not emerge from the Ego—and just as the Self gives birth to the Ego, the Ego gives birth to individual consciousness. This type of Self-sourcing, not to be confused with the pathology of dead end narcissism, consistently exposes the self (ego) to the Self. The purpose of this Self-sourcing is to find an ever-expanding Self-acceptance naturally blossoming towards greater acceptance of, and empathy, for others. To the performer this asocial process can release a greater presence of generosity through the act of a total offering of the Self.

Asocial intent can be established in several ways. One way occurs after each participant takes a pledge to become totally responsible for their own safety and creative states. This vow establishes self-accountability for one's fears and frustrations in the midst of any creative process. It also sets up a non-responsibility to others in the social sense. Asocial is not antisocial; we do not create in a socially hostile environment. Committing fully to this silent vow of self-responsibility opens the door to the vast spectrum of our Humanity within us as individuals via the energetic strata and complexes of the internal landscape. We are looking to discover ways of being, relating and doing that embraces our verticality as a foundation for more scrupulous interaction with the world, i.e., how to interact with others and the world with verticality intact.

Asocial intent can also be discovered by any heightened value assigned to the property of space itself. Expanding spatial awareness can support an asocial climate. This process can be demonstrated by directing one's attention onto the space around, below and above oneself while physically moving through space and by relating to the space between others while moving through space. Imagine a large room with many individuals moving about without relating or looking at each other but rather, engaged in the moment-to-moment process of relating only to the space between each other.

By keeping the attention on the space itself—rather than the things and people in the space—certain spatial pathways avail themselves, resulting in a more fluid group unity; picture a swarm of self-governing bodies in motion.

Any ongoing practice of spatial awareness can dramatically increase the sense of trust between people by the respect shown for each other's personal space. When we no longer relate out of fear or distrust, our more authentic selves can naturally emerge, come out to play and celebrate the freedom of being, a freedom from seeking acceptance, approval and other inhibiting social considerations.

More on paratheatre at: www.paratheatrical.com

the emotional plague

"The emotional plague" is a term initially proposed by Wilhelm Reich for the irrational insistence on beliefs and ideas that depend on dissociation of mind from body. Reich also referred to it as "the neurotic character in destructive action on the social scene". Though this body/mind dissociation has plagued humanity for centuries, it wasn't until the "The Age of Reason" that intellect was exalted to god-like status thanks to the immense success of Newton's theories and Descartes' "Meditations". Since then, the snowballing effect has gripped the collective psyche with overly-literalist thinking made even more dismal by the diminishing presence of Imagination in the culture at large. Imagination is a canary in the coal mine of the collective unconscious. Whether it's on the personal or collective levels, imagination death precedes the death of the soul.

In the current Hypermedia Era, the body/mind fissure has been dramatized via massive collective projection of vital physical, emotional, and sexual energy into mentally absorbent mediums such as the internet, VR technology, video games, mass media advertising, and too much television. If the emotional plague is maintained by constant disassociation of mind and body, we can expose the virus whenever we are mistaking the virtual for the real, or taking any image or any idea of a reality for the reality itself, where we are eating the menu instead of the meal, mistaking the map for the territory, etc.

Two modern-day symptoms of the emotional plague in the Hypermedia Era have surfaced as: 1) an increasing trend towards de-personalization, homogenization and gentrification and 2) a steadily decreasing capacity for direct experience. As we lose trust and faith in the legitimacy of firsthand experience, we can naturally become more vulnerable and compliant to the dictates of external sources of authority and its endless cycles of obedience and punishment.

Without enough trust in our own innate sensibilities, intuitions and instincts we suffer from an absence of vital information, leading to a growing incapacity to distinguish between the real from the illusory, the true from the false, and what's right from what's wrong. Without self-trust —trust in our own direct experience—we remain as timid children dependent on parental approval and guidance for the way we live, work, create and die.

What is real and what is an illusion ? Do you know ? Do you care ? If you don't know and can say so, you are probably just waking up. If you don't know and/or don't care, don't bother; you are probably fast asleep. The emotional plague doesn't care either and you will soon be assimilated, if you have not already been consumed. If you have come to know what's real in life, dare to live by your vision, your truth; your example acts as a beacon to those lost at sea in their struggle to survive as living, awakening human beings.

AHA! — P. Emerson Williams

Overcome — P. Emerson Williams

POWER

by Christopher S. Hyatt, Ph.D.

What people commonly call power is really just weakness. The power of the weak is generally thought of as the formula of the ruled and those that rule. The rulers demand to rule, and the ruled demand to be ruled. This circular mechanical process is the drying up of life, rather than the seeding of life.

It is a symbiosis of death: the feeding of the mechanical process of life that doesn't care about value and worth but only about eating and not being eaten. This mechanical quality is inherent in all living things, but the human animal has the potential to become more than its mechanical nature. Though the mechanical nature is an aspect of the Self, the Self in creating the human brain gave itself the possibility to experience itself as (subject-object) as well as the possibility for growth. This is a task few humans have taken up. Most are enmeshed in the maze of existence while thinking they are free.

The weak ego desires great shows of power and success. For the weak ego, nothing is ever enough, no amount of money, status, sex, influence, power, and so on. It is lost in its identity maze, completely concerned with country, race, religion, family, status, etc. It cannot rest, relax, drop its guard. It is always on the front lines waiting for the next opportunity to inflate itself, or fearing the next blow which will uncover the rawness of its vulnerability and pain.

Power is a force……an organic uncontrived force. When it is formulated through an authentic person, its various qualities—including its deficiencies—will appear as beauty. There is style and beauty to real power regardless of age or position in the world of people and things.

On the other hand a weak, greedy, starving ego is like a bull in a china shop: wreaking havoc wherever it goes. It is sloppy, without style, without dignity, without taste, without solid values for itself It is a pig in a feeding frenzy. It is ugly to look at. It is unaware of the world except as a breast or a great threat.

The weak ego is in constant threat and pain, expending large amounts of energy on guarding itself from humiliation, embarrassment, and fear. Many people with a weak ego will degrade themselves as a self-protective device rather than let themselves be surprised by a blow.

Others are addicted to chemicals and behaviors which gives them a false sense of security and power, while still others are aggressive and abrasive. A weak ego clings, and it is difficult for it to share itself freely and openly.

The strong ego enjoys expressing its power. It is not depressed nor suffers from incessant cravings. A person with authentic power will want to expend his power; that is, share it with the world. The strong ego is charitable, not just for the sake of giving, but to free itself from any sense of restriction. When it withholds power it is incubating, transforming, making preparations for giving birth to the New.

Unlike the weak ego which is often wounded, pained and reactive to the insults, trials and tribulations of life, the strong ego will hurt but will learn and gain from the pain. The weak ego simply desires to escape; the strong ego wishes to confront, to go deeper.

The person with a weak ego is easily bored. He doesn't have the power or the internal resources to keep himself entertained. Often the boredom transforms into depression or blind aggression.

True power resides only in the Self through its present highest expression: the man. The Self is an artist, even to the point of creating and experiencing evil and destruction, and yet it contains the seed of peace and harmony. The essence of its own Darkness is its own Self-overcoming.

In Conclusion ladies and germs we present, in the center ring, all the way from somewhere else…

Collaboration in Theory and Practice

by Joseph Matheny

This is a manifesto about collaboration—it's about the realities and functional challenges you will face trying to create and maintain a working collaboration environment. This is not one of those screeds about "collaboration and why the world's future depends on it" or anything like that. This is a meat and potatoes guide. Why I have included this is because many think that being an individualist prevents you from being able to function within a team. Many feel that this would make them a "joiner," follower, whatever. Listen up. You can collaborate for set periods of time with other like-minded individuals to accomplish great, magnificent feats of chaos, confusion and disruption. Then, TAZ style, tear down your tent and move on. There are simply some things that can be achieved with a group that are supremely difficult to impossible to achieve alone.

TOOLS

For the theory hounds:

It is only proper that such a manifesto begin with Doug Engelbart. In the 1960s, Engelbart and his laboratory at the Stanford Research Institute (SRI) invented the fundamental building blocks found in all of today's collaborative tools—everything from the data structures (hypertext) and user interfaces (windowing systems), to applications (groupware) and physical interfaces (the mouse). Engelbart's work was driven by some deceptively simple observations, which he described in his 1962 paper, "Augmenting Human Intellect: A Conceptual Framework."

[http://www.liquidinformation.org/engelbart/62_paper_top.ht ml]

There are a lot of buzzwords floating around these days that all loosely or tightly bind to the larger meta-concept of collaboration: social networks seems to be the buzz bomb du jour. My personal favorite source of information about emerging paradigms in collaboration is my old cyber-buddy Jon Lebkowsky and his blog, Weblogsky. [http://www.weblogsky.com/wfs.html]. If you're interested in really drilling down into these concepts, I'd recommend Jon L's blog as an excellent starting place. Last, but not least, you can always google one of the above terms and take it from there.

But enough of that.

Now I'm going to talk about some ideas that I have extracted from real-life experiences in group efforts and collaborative projects. No matter what you call it, it all boils down to one thing. What we are talking about here is a many to one relationship to project development and management. While this may sound simple when stated on the bottom line, it is amazingly complex and full of many potential points of failure, to put it into network management parlance. Studying networks and how they function is actually a very sound idea when planning a collaborative project. This applies to social as well as technical networks. The main thing I most often see missing from group endeavors is a sound project management plan. Let's talk about project management. A couple of things need to happen before a collaborative project is started in earnest. A conceptual for delivery should be fleshed out before you begin deployment

• A simple set of tools should be evaluated and chosen
• A schedule should be drafted and all known elements should be plotted, with milestones and deliverables marked inside of this schedule
• A core team should already be pre-qualified and selected
• Someone should be chosen to be the leader or leaders, which I always refer to as 'central command'
• It helps for projects larger in scope to have teams and therefore team leaders that report to 'central command'

These are general bullet points and you may add or subtract to fit the particular idiosyncrasies of your own particular group working. I will now take each one of those bulleted items and expand on them a bit.

This stage of planning is analogous to the draft state of a novel*. It can be as simple as an outline, a set of index cards or as complex as a Labyrinth storyboard

[http://www.habitualindolence.net/labyrinth/]

or a Brain [http://www.thebrain.com/].This can be drawn up by one person or several, and it can be taken from a pre-existing body of work or it can be created from scratch. The important thing is that you have a map, even a crude one, before you invite too many people to join your party. The barebones framework includes:

• Starting point (how does this thing begin)
• Body (what are the points that the act is trying to get across and how do we get there)
• Resolution (how does this thing end)

Next, a listing of main characters, their psychology profiles and motivations should be listed. Then, once that is done I always like to plot the characters within the storyline framework. I also like to make rough outlines of places, secondary characters, and any groups or organizations that may play a key role in the story. Personally, I like using The Brain [http://www.thebrain.com/] for this outlining because it allows me to link people, places and things together in arrangements of importance (casual to critical) and in a non-hierarchical fashion, much the way real life works, in a social sense. To address cross platform issues with other team members I have only recently began to experiment with other tools like StorySprawl [http://www.storysprawl.com/]

or Labyrinth [http://www.habitualindolence.net/labyrinth/]

Wiki [http://wiki.org/] has been immensely useful in the recent past for collaborative development and I can highly recommend it as a simple and useful tool. Other tools are as varied as your imagination, even including the trusty old private web board scenario. A nice open source solution is the ArsDigita Community System [http://philip.greenspun.com/wtr/using-the-acs.html].

This is also as good a place as any to, at least arbitrarily, come up with the mechanics of your 'belief engine.' What media are utilized and how, timing, manpower needed to actualize it, etc. It's best to leave this loose because the mechanics of your ground game need to be fluid so you can easily adapt and adjust to the dynamic landscape of 'playtime'. Good planning also recognizes the cost of over planning. Remember, you can't know it all, nor can you take into account all the circumstances that will arise once you have actual humans interacting with the abstracted user interface of your project. That brings me to an important point; this level is for all intents and purposes, although abstracted, the user interface to your narrative. Remember that. Good sources of information on approaches to this part of the process include, but are not limited to:

• Video game story line and movie script writing resources—stay away from “how to get your script greenlighted” types of guides. Look to structural guides instead.
• Multimedia story development tools and guides
• Storyboard development resources
• Human Interface, design and theory [See the earlier parts of this book and http://www.immersivegaming.com/tools.htm for a list of resources

A simple set of tools should be evaluated and chosen. It is always easier to decide on standards before you get started. This will help you avoid a lot of snags and pitfalls during the actual development and deployment processes. When at all possible, choose tools that allow for some flexibility should you wish to add more team members along the way. Lean away from proprietary or skewed solutions unless functionality absolutely dictates those proprietary solutions are the only available option. Cross platform solutions and ease of use should always be kept in mind when choosing tools for group use.

A schedule should be drafted and all known elements should be plotted, with milestones and deliverables marked inside of this schedule Ok, so this element will change as things progress but it still doesn’t hurt to have a rough idea of what it will take, time-wise, to pull off your idea. When trying to fit things into a timeline you will often times put your ideas into a concrete enough form to be able to recognize ‘feature creep’ or in some cases, feature absence. It’s really simple. Ask yourself: “How long do I want to do this and can I do everything I’ve planned on doing within that timeframe”. You may find that your scope is too ambitious or that you really don’t have the time and energy to execute all the ideas that you threw into the early planning stages. You can then adjust the timeframe or trim the ‘features’ to keep your project within the boundaries of sanity and completion. Treat your product as just that, a product. This will help with focus and staying on point. A core team should already be prequalified and selected. There are many ways to do this.

It will, of course, be impossible to have your entire team built before hand, in fact you should leave enough flex room so you can add candidates along the way as the project itself will produce ‘superusers’. Leaving yourself a little wiggle room will allow unforeseen circumstances like team leaders dropping out, being voted out, or proving to be incapable, to occur without creating a cascading failure effect in your project once it is up and going. Someone should be chosen to be the leader or leaders, which I always refer to as 'central command.'

You will always have people who will object to this principle and I'm the first to admit that a decentralized approach can work, but more often than not, it doesn't. This will also derail any power struggles that may arise later during the critical period of execution. Get it out of the way early. This is often simple because the original action-line is usually the product of one or several minds. Pick one or several flag bearers of the vision and allocate final approval or veto power to these people. There's nothing wrong with taking a democratic approach such as voting or debate but remember that there will always be times when a quick decision is needed and when that time arises, someone must be mandated to make those decisions. I am reminded of a feature film I crewed on. The director was asked if this wasn't in fact a democracy, with all of the crew, from the grips to the production designer, to the actors to the director having some say in how things get done. He replied: "Sure, I'm open to suggestions. I guess this is a democracy up until the point that I have to say no to something." Yes, I laughed too. Later when I went on to direct some music video projects on my own, I really understood what he was saying. A film project or OM style project is more like running an aircraft carrier than it is like living on a commune.

It helps for projects larger in scope to have teams and therefore team leaders that report to 'central command.' Depending on the size and scope of your project, a hierarchical structure may be appropriate. Keep in mind that groups will naturally fall into pyramidical structures, with some taking lead, others taking more of a follow posture. Those that float to the top of these natural settlings may be useful as mid-tier leaders and can even be useful as agents to recruit later. The command structure does not have to be rigid or cut off. It often helps to have an 'ear to the ground' so to speak, so keep mid-tier recruitment in mind as an option. If you ever played any of the Steve Jackson games or Flying Buffalo games, you already understand this principle.

In summation, I cannot stress enough that planning a framework for true and open collaboration may seem like a contradiction in terms, but it clearly is not. Some preliminary planning and construction of a workflow environment is integral to having a productive collaborative experience. Don't be afraid to plan but also keep in mind that as you progress and learn you will need to adjust and adapt. Building a framework allows for both while also providing a working space from which to launch a killer experience.

Now everybody join hands and sing Kumbaya. :P

Another Zending.
To be continued…

TELLING THE TRUTH AMONGST OTHER LIES

by Christopher S. Hyatt, Ph.D.

When you are told how valuable you are, and how much you are loved, be on guard, for it means a surprise. :::::::: When you are told how grateful someone is ::: be on guard. :L:L:L:

To be told anything about you means you will receive very little, as the monkey is well trained to believe how desperate people are for compliments, and they can substitute for the rawness of deeds.

:::::::: WORDS ARE NOT CASH! ::::::::

When someone tells you that they are your friend, what they are saying is they want you to be their friend :::::::: but will feel imposed on if you take them up on their offer to be your friend. ::::: Most people can not give much of themselves, nor do they want to :::: and while you smile at their compliments and their praise, watch their hands: one is holding onto their billfold and the other is grasping for yours. ::::::

Someone's need is not their sincerity, and unless it pains them to give…

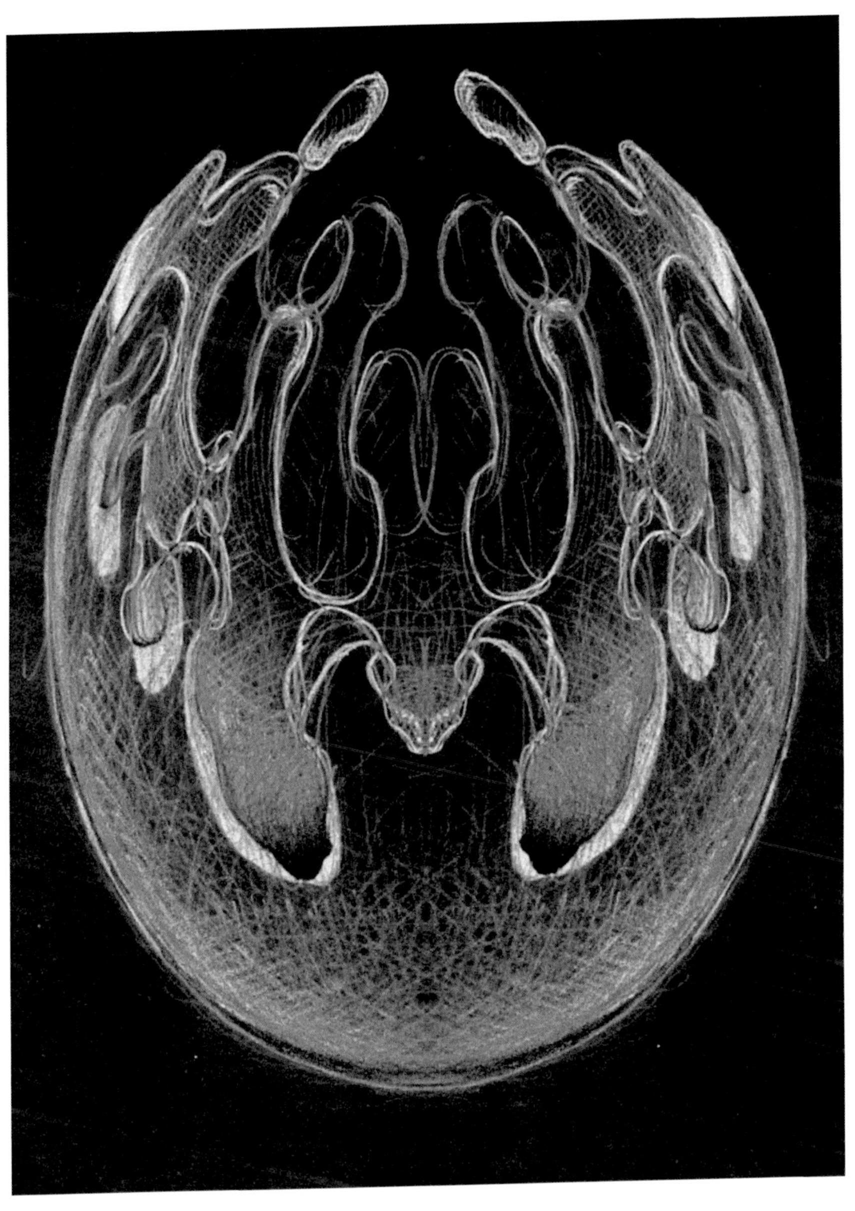

Egg — P. Emerson Williams

Incubus by MobiusFrame

We are forever turning between the almost infinite symbolizing
powers of our mind and the crucible of our factual existence.
From the expanding bubbles of our putrid cries we build
castles in the sky, hoping for salvation from our creations,
but as Wm. James has said, "the skull will grin at the banquet."
To be stronger than life itself, to say no to the setting sun,
to breathe life into life, as if tomorrow would never come.
This is the Man.

— C.S. Hyatt, Ph.D.

I HAVE UNDEIFIED EVERYTHING

by Christopher S. Hyatt, Ph.D.

I have UnDeified everything,
even Me.
Believing in Nothing,
powers now freed,
i walk through walls
finding Nothing,
except me.
I own everything that touches me.
and like a snake shed everything.
to be free, to be free, yes to be free
Yet, yearning for a prison so i willn't be me
A slave freed from gods
to live and die in this raging sea.

— C.S. Hyatt, Ph.D.
1993, In the Middle of the Pacific Ocean

DEATH IS AN ABSOLUTE
LIFE IS CONDITIONAL

All too many people are corks on the sea of life. They don't live life, they are lived by life.

The Extreme Individual Institute is dedicated to the proposition that many people can become creations of their own will for life.

Look at young children: they live life in wonder, excitement and joy. Our initial wonder, excitement and joy is defiled by parents and teachers.

The giggle must become the polite laugh, the fun must be only when appropriate, the spontaneity must be torn from our breast. Joy is replaced by drudgery and individuality surrendered to the social collective. Thus is life passed in stupidity.

As adults we can not begin anew, but we can take a solemn oath to recapture as much as possible of that joy, wonder and power we were born with.

To exist is easy—to live is an accomplishment.

We dedicate this little book to the those among you who are willing to live the full life.

We invite you to join with us in a journey into the wonder of life. To those we say: seas however high and a bountiful journey.

BECOME WHO YOU ARE—
THERE ARE NO GUARANTEES

— Christopher S. Hyatt, from the Western Lands